KERNELS OF CORN

KERNELS OF CORN

Christian Langston Davidson

T.E.D. Ministries
PRESS
Saint Louis

KERNELS OF CORN

Cover art: "Waters Under the Heavens," by Greg Moore, watercolor; commissioned for this publication.

Published by:
T.E.D. Ministries Press
P.O. Box 34041
St. Louis, MO 63134
www.tedministries.com

ISBN 978-0-9786616-0-1

Library of Congress Control Number: 2008900697

Printed in United States of America.

for the gospel of my Savior
Jesus Christ
with all my love

in memory of
Pastor Harold Clark
&
Sister Peggy Clark

Foreword

"Why poetry?" Perhaps some or many of you may be wondering that question. It seems that most whom God has gifted with a ministry in Christ's church produce song and music, or preach, or work with their hands. What contribution to the mission of Christ do I expect to make by publishing poetry?

First, most song is a form of poetry—poetry put to music. And music is perhaps the mightiest influence in the Church, outside of love. Second, our Bible contains what many consider the greatest collection of poetry ever compiled: the Book of Psalms. The books of Proverbs, Ecclesiastes, and Song of Songs (or Song of Solomon) are also generally considered poetry. In addition, I would suggest that the Book of Job is both a morality play and a dramatic poem. I also find the books of Isaiah and Revelation very poetic.

What is poetry? Many, writers and critics alike, have proffered reasonable definitions through the centuries, even though—like God—it may be impossible to define precisely. Just as everyone that knows God has a personal and unique relationship with Him, everyone has a personal understanding of what poetry is.

To me, poetry is not about rhyme, meter, form, length, syntax, or any of the devices found in many poems (I suggest that a poem is not poetry, but an attempt to capture poetry). I think poetry is a unique and creative way of seeing this world and this life God has created. For most of us, I imagine, this world and this life have a tendency to become rather routine—mostly black and white. Poetry is a departure from routine, artistic splashes of color. I believe God has given me a gift to recognize and appreciate poetry and to craft that recognition and appreciation into poems. That would make me a poet.

Yes, a poet—that's what I am. When I consider what I'm best at, I'm not a singer, I'm not a musician, I'm not a preacher, I'm not a missionary, but I'm a poet. And, as Paul instructs us in Colossians 3, I do what I do—as a poet—heartily for the Lord (vv. 17, 23). Just as the Psalms inspire and comfort many and the Proverbs teach, it is my prayer and desire that the results of my attempts to capture poetry will serve a good purpose or two. I seek to edify my fellow believers and to preach the Gospel of Jesus Christ by what I do best. That's what this book is about: enjoy!

Christian Langston Davidson

P.S. Underneath some poems you will see some comments in a typeface like this one. (This is supposed to represent my handwriting. Frankly, it's not. Believe me, you wouldn't want to try to read my actual handwriting: "hieroglyphics" is one of the nicer things it's been called!) I thought I would include these comments to help make the poems more meaningful to you without detracting from the wholeness of the individual poems themselves.

The Service

At Your Service 3

Reign Dance Prayer 4

How I Know God Is King of All the Earth 5

Praise Offering 6

Maxim no. 51: Worship 7

My Soul Worships..8

Kiss 9

Breezy 11

Saving the Sparrow 13

The Art of the Gospel..15

The Pastor 19

The Transfusion 21

The Garden of My Soul 24

The Chocolate Comet 25

From the Journal of a Novice Director: 27

Celestial Screenplay..29

Account of Calvary 32

The Lemming's Testimony 34

Poetic License 36

Burnt-out Bulb 37

River of Light...38

The Greatest River 39

The Call of Fireflies 41

Follow the Leader

Just a Little Talk with 47

Pledge of Obedience Prayer...50

Salvation Acceptance Speech 51

Sign 52

The Esteem Poem 54

The Sponge 56

Go With the Flow 57

Worth Remembering 58

The Voice of Eden...59

Follow in the Trailblazers Footsteps 60

A Prayer to Follow 61

First Steps 63

Walking Prayer......65
Jigsaw Puzzle Prayer......66
Bringing the Flashlight to Its Knees 67
Peaceful Rest......68
At the End of the Night......69
Closet Fire......71
Opening......72
Morning Coffee......73
Maxim no. 44: Service......74
The Waiter......75
This Morning 76
Coffee House Prayer 77
Ritual Suicide......79

Enjoy the Journey

In the Zone 83
Home Court Advantage......84
How the Champion Climbs the Rock 86
Promise, No Idle Threat 87
Extreme High Hurdles 88
How the Champion Is Champion......89
Missing the Boat 91
The Cat's Tale 92
The Old Dog's Tale 93
The Glove......95
Blowing Kisses Back 97
Poet Laureate of the Swamp 98
The Larva 100
Dedicated to a Dying Tree 101
Colonels of Corn 102
Prayer from a Fiery Furnace 103
Words of the Last One In 105
The Reporters......107
How the Champion Lives 108
The Story of a Great Journey 110
Spirits Rising......114
High Hurdles 115

I was glad when they said unto me, "Let us go into the House of the Lord." — Ps. 122:1

One

The Service

Let's go to church!

At Your Service

Everyone please have a seat.
I'm Christian; I will be serving you today
Our specials? Actually there's only one true item on the menu:
Jesus Christ, a.k.a. The Truth,
The Bread of Life and the Living Water
More and better nutrition than you can find in any culinary establ-
  lishment in town

In fact, why don't you stand:
Up on your feet and stretch out your arms
Better to serve God if you are in position to receive Him.
While you are waiting, clap your hands in anticipation
Talk loudly about how much you're looking forward to this meal
'Cause you know it's going to be good as soon as you taste it
Just as food critic king David said in the eighth bite of his 34th
  visit.

Take your time
I'll go to the kitchen and talk to the
Chef, who's making preparations for you now.
Feel free to call out when you're ready to order.

Reign Dance Prayer

Lord
    of this dance,
Let everyone who hears these words
Be free to celebrate with dancing feet and clapping hands
For You reign, Lord God,
Over us all with a loving and merciful hand
Whether we realize we are subject to Your rule or not.

Please give us free rein to caper and frolic along the trail.
But if we start to stumble or stray from the path
Pull the straps tight and take up the slack.

Direct our romp through the course
Leading us to leap over every obstacle
So we can stand,
Heroes at the finish line
Where flowers and shouts will rain down on us
As we share in Your eternal victory.

How I Know God Is King of All the Earth

One glad morning
I was opening the eastward blinds of the building where I work
 securely
And I saw a squirrel sitting on an electric pole climbing peg
It was looking north, watching the rising sun,
Alert, with furry tail saluting at attention

My first thought was
          Praise the Lord!

It had to be me receiving telepathic communication
From the squirrel (since animals can't talk)
And if a fuzzy rodent with an acorn brain
Can praise the Lord who created the sun
To give life to every level of the food chain,
Then we top-link humans ought to extol Him vociferously.
          All hail the King!

Praise Offering

When I pick up my instrument,
Possessed by the hypnotic inspiration of my Muse,
Who is so good
He makes me better,
And I leap for joy boldly into
Da Zone,

Squiggles of ink dance off their page
Words become exultant shouts
Sounds flow into a sonorous melody

And every dark spirit in the belly of the world quakes
Fearing that on the day they think they rule the earth
Someone will open this book
And the sweet incense will waft out,
Choking the very hellish air they inhabit
With God's glorious cloud

All it takes is three little lines, just twelve small words:
     I praise God
     For His Son
     Died to save us from sin!

Written October 31

Maxim no. 51: Worship
John 4:23, 24

A spirit in worship of the Father
Cannot be contained
Because God cannot be contained.

Strike the gong
Let its sonorous vibrations
Bubble over into your soul, mind, and body
'Til you express uncontainable joy.

My Soul Worships
Psalm 150

And it's still ringing!

How wonderful
Voices in concert
Harmonizing joyously,
Tambourines rattling vigorously;
Piano resounds with musical laughter
As a worshipper of the Holy One
Tickles the ebonies and presses the ivories.
A flute atop the melody tree warbles like a mockingbird while
Trumpets blare, saxes bleat like lambs
Guitar strings hum along, and the bass
It rides down low, supporting
While the platoon of drums
Calls out an upbeat cadence
Then

[GONG CRASH] **PRAISE**

(repeat)

Kiss

My God
You are no genie
(Infinitely more powerful and caring)
But I wish I could
Press my lips against Your cheek

You
Shower kisses upon me

I feel kissed when I see the rising sun blow color towards the horizon
I feel kissed when I hear wonderful music smack vibes into the air
I feel kissed when I taste the sweetness of chocolate melt on my tongue
I feel kissed when I stop and smell the roses' ambrosial incense
I feel kissed when I catch a cool sunny breeze rub like velvet on my skin
And even when my loved ones pucker up and lay one on me

I can pucker up and return the favor with my loved ones,
But can I reach up and take the
Wind in my arms, dip it, and press it with my kisser?

Your tokens of love to me are multitudinous
Like the grains of sand in the Sahara
Like the stars in the Alaskan sky
Like the drops of water in the Indian Ocean
(I'm sure You've already heard every line and cliché I could use).
You must be crazy about me,
Especially since You gave up the only Son You ever begat
To teach me how to be a member Your family:
It makes me blush!

Well, I want to express my love, too

So Big Brother won't get jealous and I get in trouble.
Let Big Bro come and teach me how to pucker up and smooch
And let my effort make You blush.

Breezy
for the Riverview Church of God music ministry
which I dub The Breeze of Joy

They feel
the rhythm of the march of spring
steppin' in the breezes

Their wing tips rufflin',
tail feathers bouncin',
feelin' the cool warm breezes
takin' over the land.

Breezy
this thing goes,
the march of spring.
May have been cold yesterday
but migrating from the south are birds of all kinds
Ridin' a tidal wave of warm breezes.

Flutey sounds of songbirds
claim the land they'll call home.
They sit, perch on the tree
open their beaks,
lift their lilting voices
in honor of the Creator of all song.

I feel
the rhythm of the march of spring
steppin' warm in the breezes

My fingers twitchin'
toes tappin'
diggin' the warm breezes
takin' over my bod.

• • •

Driven by the eaglelion's mighty flap,
joy in tow
migrating back to the north.

Joy fills up the warm breezes
My soul
like a kite
bobs up and down in the rising march wind
like a syncopated jazz strain

I feel
My own call to claim the warm spring joy
as my territory
so I lift my own voice
in honor of the Creator of all song.

Saving the Sparrow

There I was, the security guard
At an inn not quite ready for occupation
And you, poor sparrow,
Were trapped inside, resting on a sill,
Exhausted from repeated attempts to flee
From that tremendous prison of technology.

I knew you couldn't escape through delusions.
You could see your freedom,
But your wings couldn't carry you to it
When you continually smacked into
What you couldn't see.

And I came for you, but you were afraid.
You frantically resumed your way out
And continued to be blocked
Then you turned around, and your new flight
Collided with another delusion
Oh! I feared for you,
But you reversed again at my next approach
And bumped your head again.
I had to wear you out.

Why didn't you trust me?
I knew the way through the maze
And I was there to take you though the portal.
Anyway, here we go together, blessed.
You seem stunned—
Disoriented from your ordeal?
Or surprised that you're in no danger
Perched on my hand?

Ah, there you fly
And safely ascend into a tree

But we have shared something unique and treasured.
Though you may never comprehend this rescue
Your chirps and songs bear your freedom, so
Our tender communion
Will forever whisper though
Legendary trees.

Based on a true story – my own!

The Art of the Gospel

one

Public Service Announcement:

Unfriendly waters rain upon the earth frequently, and
The world is frequently pockmarked by holes
Breaches, slits, cracks, ditches, rifts
Fissures, ruts, crevices, gorges, pits
Canyons, gulfs, abysses:

Still, every slip and fall in a rainstorm doesn't have to dive,
Doesn't have to plummet into a depression
A depression so deep, so bottomless
That by the time you ever
Reach bedrock, irresistible gravity will make you
Leave a grand impression on the devil of oppression

So before the next time you find it raining oily,
Liquid ice,
Protect yourself from the potential of a perilous plunge:
Take notes on the seminar:
Principles of
The Anatomy of a Comeback.

two

The Anatomy of a Comeback
One Poet's Portrait of the Savior

Begin with the feet. Four of them.
The talons are retracted (pray you don't have to see them)

And the tough, callused pads of these paws never twitch
Not even when pierced by thorns.

Move upward to study the legs:
Lean, with a slight bulge of powerful muscles
Now survey the tail, featuring
Five long rich-brown feathers
They spread to give balance and swivel for maneuverability.
The back: flexible, archable, but the bones are unbreakable
Just enough fat around the spine to
Nourish the entire superior organism and
Provide cushioned support for any rider.

Now bring your eyes around and slide your view up to his breast
Broad, a tremendous thumping heart resides there.
And just a little higher and a little further back
You'll find the finest plumes ever woven together,
Forming a long, pulsating wing.
There's another one on the other side of this
Perfectly symmetrical being
Together they oscillate in harmonious rhythm and
Generate awesome lift with just a single determined stroke
And these wings spread wide, allowing the freedom to soar for-
   ever.

Riders of this majestic royal thoroughbred can run their hands
Up his strong back over soft neck feathers and around to his
Bold chin held always at an angle higher than the horizon.
When this king opens his mouth, it's usually to roar
Or screech in anger at one of the world's injustices
And that's when you'll see those teeth!
Dozens, all shaped like sharp beaks made perfect for
Ripping apart offensive, insubordinate beasts.
Oh, you'd much rather hear the soothing sound of his
Purring throat, indicating his approval of those
Lambs which follow the shepherd.

• • •

Finally, notice the eyes, but don't dare stare too hard
Those extremely keen eyes
Beam an intense singular beam that never wavers
And the gaze is always upward, towards the rising sun.

three

The One to Call On:

It's the eaglelion
Who you have glimpsed through a portrait of words
He is out there, nearby,
Hovering outside the confines of light visible to humans

Whenever you feel your spirits falling
Reach your mindflight back to your notes on this
Non-crash course on the Anatomy of a Comeback
Which you have just gone through.

If you have listened to and believed my lecture and passed the
 course
You'll be able to reconstruct on your mental canvas
The powerful visage of the champion,
Fierce towards wolves, compassionate towards sheep

You'll remember
And call out His name
Then, on a wing and a prayer, your
Deliverer will come to you
You'll see Him, like a towering pillar

He'll take you on His back, fly you out of your deluged abyss
Through a rainbow and land you
In a land of the phoenix nouveau sun.

17

You'll have a chance
To dry off and stand on solid ground.

The Pastor

Inspiration fell heavy upon
A sheepkeeper in the Quarath Plains one night.
Hit his head so hard he started preaching to the sheep:

You heard about The Shroud and want to see what
Jesus looked like?
I'll do you one better than that
How'dja like to meet Him *right now*?

Stop trembling, silly, you're in no danger.
I'm no wolf in shepherd's clothing planning to
Devour you, prematurely send you to heaven

No, no
I just want to introduce you to Jesus, personally.
Take your Bible; hold it in your right hand
Your *Holy* Bible, the Book of books
Comprising the Word of the Voice Supreme,
The Anthology whose title is an acronym for
Basic Instructions Before Leaving Earth
(I'm not making this up!)
Got it? Okay — you're shaking hands with Jesus right now.

Behold the awesome changing power of Christ
He was with God before ever the earth existed.
Then He was the Word which created life as we know it,
Starting with four compact words none of us was around to hear at
 the time.
Next we hear that He was a Voice walking through His garden
Telling a smooth-tongued beguiling snake
He'd sentence Himself to be restrained in the form of a man
Who would footstomp his hissing head
(Don't look at me so funny
Ain't no English major that can fully diagram that sentence

Or completely conjugate that action verb).

In the meantime He became a massive cloud on a mountaintop
And wrote Himself onto a rock tablet
To be carried around in a paragraphernacle . . .
Ahem! I mean to say He was testimony
That rode in an ark in a tabernacle.

Later He appeared to a prophet as a small voice very still
In a chariot driven by wind, earthquake and fire:
After you let all the uproar parade by
You have to lean in real close and be real still to hear Him.

When you do, you'll hear His matchless wisdom,
Which the proverbial king cast as a woman
Standing outside the city proclaiming
That she loves those who love her and that
Those who get up early to look for her will find her.

In His greatest statement He's hanging on a cross saying nothing
Nothing, that is, but forgiveness for the rogue sheep who mangled
 Him.
Man, that's one powerful dangling modifier!
While floating up to heaven, He stretched out and maimed that
 snake
As eleven dedicated students stood by taking note.
He sent down empowering winds of change that blow
When you speak His towering name.

All that remains of His body,
Which has been bread for wanderers in a strange land, manna
Has been sculpted into the collected words you just shook hands
 with.
So I conclude with these basic instructions:
Before you leave this earthly life
Get to know Jesus by reading Him.

The Transfusion

one

Diagnosis

The patient:

There's something wrong with my face, isn't there?
Might as well be honest.
Ain't a pretty sight.
Know I been singed in a smelting oven
Yet that son of a devil called me paleface

I'm embarrassed.
I'd blush, but my red blood cells
Lack the iron will to stand.
I must have amnesia— I mean anemia.
Now that I mention it, I feel dizzy
Think I'll go lie down
'Til I start at the shouts of trumpets.

Hmm, my family physician, the good
Dr. R. Ah Fica
Who's not lost any patient who came to him,
Says my condition can be treated easily
All I need is a transfusion
And before I know it I'll be on my feet
Pushing my bed down the hospital hall
With another victim of the war in it.

• • •

two

Prognosis

The Physician:

Be still. This procedure will not cause you
Any more discomfort than you already feel in your moment of
  weakness.
Why should you be squeamish? It's not you who bled seven pints
After being whipped, punctured with a thorny mock crown
Nailed three times and pierced in the side
As if I had some unrighteous behavioral disorder.

No, no, don't squirm; smile
I'm not telling you these things to rub your face in a guilt trip
That would be a bedside manner unworthy of me.
No, I buried that dead stuff and left it behind.
I'm telling you my story to let you know that
When this procedure is complete, you will be a new and stronger
  person

Because if I can do what no other living thing has ever done:
Will myself out of the grave with no blood in me
And am yet living thousands of years later—
Then surely just one microscopic drop of the blood that used to be
  in me
And is also yet living
Will proliferate in your bloodstream and correct your genetic disor-
der.

Take some time, patiently, and study the materials I've left for you
And exercise like I have always told you,
So that your renewed blood flows faster and stronger through your
  heart
And one day you'll notice how much more vibrant and full of color

you've become
And that nothing turns your stomach or makes you faint
Even though some of the minor discomfort you felt before
My healing touch sent your disorder into remission still nags you

Stand fast, now
I have given you my unfailing prognosis.

The Garden of My Soul

Matt. 13: 3-8;18-23

The Gardener of my soul
Tends the garden
Using a mysterious, but highly sophisticated technique
Medical technology will never comprehend:

A fiery wind flows unscorchingly through my body
Sowing seeds, kernels, and even coffee beans
In the garden of my soul

If any get caught up in my gastro-intestinal channel,
The pigeon-bacteria will swallow them up
And get washed down the drain.
I pray that doesn't happen.

If any get lodged in my epidermal layer
They'll germinate like itchy hair-sprouts
But then flake away like fingernails and dried-up skin.
I pray that doesn't happen.

If any find their way to my brain
And swim in the ebb and flow of my flood of thoughts
They'll become tumorous growths.
I pray that doesn't happen.

What I pray does happen is that every time
I hear the sound of the desert wind that doesn't burn
Or see the white-hot flame that doesn't blind me,
Those sowed seeds plant root in my heart,
Nourish me through the cross-pollination of my blood
And bloom in the air I exhale past my larynx.

The Chocolate Comet

Don't know 'bout you, but
My soul is a train,
And, Good Lord willing, it continuously
Runs a 12-stop route around the world.

Generally, this train carries no passengers, only freight
But now, while the load is light,
I invite you to take a ride along the scenic route
Between Station 8 and Station 9

All aboard!
At Station 8, step out of that stifling heat and humidity.
Come on in, where it's air-conditioned,
The view clear as a shooting star.
Before you get too comfy, though,
Let me take you up front to meet the engineer . . . .

You might want to shield your eyes inside the engine room
The glow in there is like a thicket full of fireflies.
But have no fear
The only thing you'll feel is a cool warmth like silk
And you may experience partial memory loss
As images that will make you smile or laugh float through your
 mind;
That's just our fireman
Who provides the train power and keeps it going in the right direc-
 tion,
According to instructions from the engineer,
Whom you won't actually see in the room
Because he is greater than the train.
And you can be sure that his hand steadies this train when nec-
 essary.

The ride to Station stop 9 is slightly uphill

As our travel takes us to a cooler altitude.
Fireman glows brighter and brighter
And the miles zip by in a blur
Like gravity pulling time, not the train

The tracks seem to no longer vibrate underneath us.
Look out the window, passengers
Let your sight drop into the speckled darkness . . .
The Chocolate Comet is hurtling through God's awesome cosmos

Relax, now,
This train has made this trip over two dozen times
And commissioned for at least seventy years of service.
You are safe as a gift-wrapped toy train in a Bethlehem manger.
You are free to get out of your seat and
Float through the poetic inkyness of the entertainment car.
You are invited to let your most pleasant thoughts aloose from your
 head
To mingle with others' to fill up the blank space
And create a collage mural for all the world to see.

✿

Written in August 1995.

From the Journal of a Novice Director: Getting Closer to the Movie's Star

Dusk,
Just finished another long, hard day of work
Knowing always that my true Boss, unseen,
Is watching me.

He bids me leave from the "office" this evening
At the right time to spot Venus and Jupiter shining bright
In a light patch of going-down-of-the-sun sky
Full of orange-tinged clouds and jet-trails
Hovering like burnt-smoke volcano fumes
Not menacing, however.

Ah, another beautiful sunset only God can stage.
Wouldn't this picturesque scene be perfect for my documentary?
I walk quickly to my car:
Good thing I keep binoculars religiously on the back seat,
'Cause now my peculiar habit will help me get closer
To this blessing for my eyes.

I lift the double-sided telescoping lenses to my face,
The November Wind nips at my bare hands with hawk's beaks,
Making me feel a delightful tingling.
The silhouette of a balding tree looms between Venus and my eyes
But there aren't enough leaves remaining to obstruct my view
So my eyes drink in the bigger and brighter light of the second
 planet.

Next I turn my gaze upward, south at an angle
To explore Jupiter
But on my way my eyes alight upon another pinpoint of light
Which I had not seen with my unaided eyes:
Faint, somewhat reddish — Mars, perhaps?

• • •

Mmmm! Three planet jewels lined up in a row,
A stargazer poet's dream picture
My mind's eye's snapping pictures like a
Camera at a basketball game where tongue-wagging Air Jordan
Is elevating for a posterizing slam-cam jam.
My soul absorbs it like Kodak Colorwatch™ film.

Suddenly I notice a detail I'd never before seen while watching the
 heavens.
My eyes had been climbing all over the hills and rocks of a jet trail
Proclaiming "This skyscape is a world in the sky"
Pulling my wandering mind-in-a-carriage all over it
Until the branches of the silhouetted tree framing Venus reached
 out
Towards my lenses, startling me upright

"Hey, aren't you supposed to be flat—a mere shadow?"
But my vision dances in and out, back and forth,
Weaving through the tree
Ecstatic
This powerful vision-enhancer not only brings me closer to the
 heavens,
It increases the three-diminsionality of my sight,
Thus the reality of things.

Now, as I develop the film
My vision in 3-d has shown me
The reality of things:
My Boss is the director/producer.
He runs the show and gets top billing
And I am a stagehand in this universal interactive movie.

✿

The view in St. Louis, Mo., on November 9, 1995.
Decipher this puzzle! Just one hint: what do you think the binoculars
symbolize?

28

Celestial Screenplay

Over the weekend
The Lord treated me to an optical love poem
In the form of cosmic art theater

Stanza 1 The first day of spring
The landscape still barren after
Hiding from winter's chill
[The curtain goes up/God removes the cover shrouding
 His latest masterpiece]
The snow in the sky finally melts away.
The Hale-Bopp comet,
The new kid in the celestial family,
Finally gets the chance to dazzle the crowd with its
 stuff.
With a sweep of its long, streaming, wispy tail
It rebuffs the attempt from the near-full moon to steal
 its glory

(A skeptic in the audience,
Unable or unwilling to suspend his disbelief,
Scientifically jeers
"It's merely a cold gaseous space rock, which,
When heated by radiation from the sun as it passes by
Appears to have a tail because of its gaseous emis-
 sions."
Astronomy professors of the world
Should return to their complex mathematical equations
Until they realize that the Creator of our universe
Uses paints, brushes, canvases, media, materials and
 apparatus
Beyond anything we mere mortals can imagine
When He creates His works of Art.
The response from us stargazers was so warm
We had summer for a day in the middle of March.)

Stanza 2   A beautiful, crisp clear evening
(The usually much-admired warm glowing sunset play
  at dusk
Was ignored while we stood in line, eagerly anticipating
  the comet's encore)
The comet appeared in the northwest
Shining like a diamond star followed by a crowd-cloud
  of
Flowing prayers and praises
(Even more brilliant this time,
The comet is like the bright star that announced the
  First Coming
Two millennia ago,
Only now it's picked up a long tail of vaspors of adu-
  lation.   {vapors? vespers?}
The crowd response was cooler than it was on opening
  night,
But some of us appreciated it anyway.
Besides, these pictures of motion had great special ef-
  fects.)

Stanza 3   Closing night
(After cruising smoothly the first two nights,
The show is now skating)
Jealous full moon, the villain,
Partially eclipses the stage in a fit of rage.
Ducking into the shadow of the earth,
It begins going through phases
Getting eaten by a dark cloud
Until it looks like a picture of Mars with only one polar
  icecap,
Its pocked face blushing devilish red under a sliver of a
  bright white hat.
It is trying to become a comet itself,
Only it has a flat head and a
Fat, dull, looping stunted tail.

30

Then, realizing that it's actions are doomed lunacy,
The moon emerges from the shadows and
Gets stampeded by an army of white noise as it covers
  the sky stage.

(I felt sharply the chill in the air as the moon made its
  cameo
After I'd arrived too late closing night to see
A third presentation of the comet's performance.
It was a once-in-a-lifetime production,
And I recommend that everyone try to see it.)

❁

St. Louis, Mo., March 24, 1997, after a spectacle in the sky.

Account of Calvary

Luke 23:32-43

I hung on a cross nearly 2000 years ago.
No, don't misunderstand me:
Three crosses in a row at Calvary
On the ends hung two scum of the earth
In between they crucified the One with the power and
Authority to save Himself and me, too

Looking out on the scene as I suffered
I couldn't understand what I was seeing
Cold-hearted people, refusing to believe
All that their King had personally shown and told them
   for three years,
Killing Him in a fit of jealous rage.

I suppose it would've been easy enough for me
To have been down there with them
If it weren't for the fact that
I was wearing my shame on my back and
It towered over me, holding me a few feet off the ground.

In my left ear I heard the wretch-like-me
On the other side of the Victim
Spew more words of doubt at Him.
Challenging Him to demonstrate the power He said He has
And to gingerly, magically remove Himself and us from our
 crosses

I knew it was too late for that—
You can goad a goat but not a God—
Hadn't this man told us to bear our cross and follow Him?
Well, there we were, just as the Script directed

Through my sweat and tears of agony

I summoned sound to my parched throat
And signified the wretch-like-me, saying
    Man, don't you fear God,
    Considering you ain't in no better shape right now!
Then my voice choked off in hoarseness
And I muttered faintly the memorable words
That many would read for the next two hundred decades
    We, indeed, have been condemned justly,
    For we are getting what we deserve for our deeds,
    But this man has done nothing wrong.
Though I cannot remember what I did wrong
Because I've done so many things wrong.

Now every day I must go through a ritual suicide,
Remembering my cross experience
And struggling with every moment to recall the words
I heard myself saying next.

Jesus, remember me when You come in Your Kingdom.

The Lemming's Testimony

I'm a pretty innocent, harmless creature,
Not a threat or hazard to anyone
Yet valued no more than a rodent.
Yeah, I do have a few natural enemies
Owls, snakes, weasels, and the like,
But it's only because they seek to devour me
Not because I ever provoke them in any way.

So with naturally good attributes like these,
Why would I need this Christmas Hero
I've heard so much about?

• • •

Whenever the winter blues blast in full swing,
And a hawk swoops down 100 miles per hour
To lacerate my back
While I run,
Uncamouflaged on a path of snow and ice,
A vulture circling overhead awaiting my demise
Somehow keeping sight of me through the
Stark raving blizzard that blinds me to its pristine possibilities
Because I can't see the snow for the flakes,

Then my heritage, which brought me up here
During an autumn with a fruitful harvest,
Can no longer nourish me,
And it comes time to run
Fast.
I've got to get out of here.

If the spirits of the elders can be believed—
And my instincts are to accept it—
My destiny is a steep nosedive

Into a swirling drink of noxious brine.
After that, the message from my ancestors' dreams goes blank

Is it my heritage to give up on pursuing the end of my dreams, or
Suicide?
I guess I do have some undesirable traits, after all
And I'm in need of a miracle Christmas Gift now
To save me from myself.

✸

Written Christmas Eve.

Poetic License

I had dug a hole for myself
In the Valley of Lethargy—
A chasm (you know I can dig 'em deep)—
And I was tottering on the edge,
Near ready to plummet into the depression
When a gift from a supreme being
Took firm hold of my collar
And gently pulled me to safety.

I heard a powerful voice say
    When I snap my fingers
    You'll roar back
    From this phantom-like state,
    Riding on the back of the
    Eaglelion soaring summer-high
    In the intense, clear air.

When I finished writing
I could only say
Thank you.

Burnt-out Bulb

Picture a burnt-out light bulb
Filament no longer pulsating with glowing energy,
Dangling like a worn-out dog's tongue
No electricity completing a circuit, flowing back to its source
Absolutely useless, ready to be tossed in the trash.

I was, once, burned out like a dead light bulb
Filament not glowing with pulsating energy
But, fortunately, I was not manufactured by
Westinghouse, GE, or Sylvania
No, I was created by a Light brighter than a thousand stars.

So, for a while I was a burnt-out dead bulb
Filament forgetting to be an energy pulse,
Shine for the whole world's benefit
But by a miracle and by grace
I was saved from being deposited in the garbage.

Now I'm not a burnt-out, dark bulb
My filament glows bright with an energetic pulse
Erasing shadows and reaching out in all directions
For that all-bright all-star
That with a quick turn, snapped my filament back in place.

River of Light

Light flows through the burning bulb
A geyser of living, irresistible energy
Fills up any space and
Drowns out shadowy figures.

Ever since those first four Voiced Words
In the beginning,
It has flowed on two wavelengths —
An optical liquid, and an unseen,
Deeper substance which catches up
The life of the victorious in its stream —
And no dark forces will ever find a shutoff valve.

Some of that light flowed through a fountain
And splashed on the page you're reading.

The Greatest River

The Nile is nifty, spilling over copious fruit in due season
The Amazon is powerful, quick to move you far
Don't call the Huang He yellow or its people, 'cause it's
    Sure to take them high
The mighty Mississippi takes no mess and gives no misery
The Danube makes people sing
Murray and its Darling are dear to their aboriginal people
The Zaire is a jewel flowing into the sunset
Saint Lawrence is great for travel
Orinoco is tropical, a fresh place to visit
The Euphrates and Tigris are twin branches in a land of choice

But ain't none of these got nothin' on the river I'm talkin' 'bout!
My man Langston said he'd known rivers—
Well, I hope and pray he knew this river:

The River of Atonement is clear blood,
Waters like radiation beyond the spectrum of visible light
Cascading upon me from a place higher than the sky

I rise and wash in it and
Tingling, it sterilizes my flesh.
The outer layers burn away
And a sweet-smelling savory smoke rises up the river

All that remains is invisible to human eyes.
Nevertheless I know my mindflight is there
On the same wavelength with the waterlight from above
It is immersed in the water alive
And connected by unbreakable submolecular bond.

My mindflight remains tethered to my body like a kite
Until it is consumed by the fatal flames of a ritual suicide.
Once the burnt offering is accepted,

All the flesh melted away like fat in the
Fiery waves of bloodlights
Releasing the perfumey vapors that
Delight angelic nostrils like a breath of fresh cool morning air,
Then my mindflight can rise like a hot-helium balloon
Without ballast—no longer under the law of gravity

Talk about exhilaration!
The currents hit the earth a thousand times harder than thunderous
 rain
With the ability to rip off all the flesh of anyone who
Selects to make the sacrifice of setting foot into the cool blazing
 blood-red tide
Yet my incorporeal mindflight floats up against the grain
Like surfing in reverse with a righteous tan.
It's an adventurous ride I look forward to
Every morning when I sit down for coffee.

The River of Atonement is cosmic
All of earth's solar system is like a guppy in its midst
But you won't be wetted by a single infrared drop
Unless you make that choice

Consider yourself invited
Join me for a ride on the river
What follows is the most fantastic voyage you can imagine.

The Call of Fireflies

If your mind were your mouth
You have sat at a king's feast; I hope you're fully satisfied
And if your eyes were your mind
You've been stargazing in admiration at the
Most dazzling bejeweled nighttime sky.

You know the story,
Years ago there was a miraculously bright star
Centered over Bethlehem.
Some pretend not to know what happened to it.
It was a comet with a fantastic train of a tail
It landed on the heart of this world
(What in the heavens would make such a
Spectacular celestial body
Wallow on our dusty planet?
It would be like Ol' Sol becoming Luna!
It was a star-crossed sacrifice.)

Anyway, you know the story
The Star of Jacob no longer dwells on earth
It ascended back into the heavens
Don't you see it?
If not, you must still be on this world,
Because the earth's dusty atmosphere obscures the view.
Rest assured that the stars you can see
From the soil of the world's deserts, lawns, beaches—
They are able to see the Star of Jacob
Quite clearly from their place above the world,
For the Star's glory encompasses the cosmos.

See a shooting star
This is a star willing to leave the sky pasture and
Hang around in the fields of earth for the harvest.
It does not return to dust,

But becomes a firefly

Some fireflies are stars that shot back to earth
To be a gatherer on behalf of the Light
Because there are grains on earth that should be stars near Glory
Are you one of them?

When you see a firefly
Stop what you're doing and focus on its communication
It's calling you to come to the Light
Rise up from the ground,
No more time for rolling in mud anymore
Find the fire that's within your belly
Light it up and you'll rise above the world.

Some fireflies are stars risen from the earth, shooting towards
 heaven
They have recognized the voice of the Light
And are in route to the pasture in the sky.

Come, the sky awaits.

✿

Consider "The Call of Fireflies" your altar call. If you know Jesus
Christ as your Lord and Savior, I rejoice with you and invite you to
turn the page and rejoice further with me.

If you don't yet know Jesus as Lord, I invite you now to allow me
to introduce Him to you. The poems in the following section attempt to
demonstrate some of the components of trusting Christ as a guiding friend.

But no one is going to force you. That is not God's will or desire. If
you find in your heart that you are not yet ready to take this step, don't

worry, I won't be offended. I understand what you're going through.
I invite you to continue reading and enjoy the poems as poems. As "At
Your Service" says, "Feel free to call out when _you're ready._"

Let us run with patience the race that is set before us, looking to Jesus, the author and finisher of our faith. — Heb. 12:1,2

Two

Follow the Leader

We can go on like this forever!

Just a Little Talk With
The Kingdom's Premier Artist and Fashion Expert

Oh. . .
Hi Emmanuel!
Lord, I'm embarrassed and ashamed:
Here you are, the
Artist of my finished portrait
And you stood at my door and knocked
And I came to the door wearing these filthy skins.
I'm very sorry.

Please
Come in and make yourself at home
I'll clean up so that you'll be comfortable.
Excuse me.

I'm tired of looking in my mirror and
Seeing a wretched soul looking back at me
Head hanging low or chin held high,
Eyes drooping at my feet or sneaking glances to my left.
And the clothes! They all are tattered,
Fit poorly, have holes, or stains.

Is that your portrait of me you hung on the wall?
Wow!
This portrait model would like to change places with the
Model portrait

You have portrayed me as a prince
A bright smile no one can deface
A glistening silver tongue
Eyes that shine like candles
A spotless, sparkling crown on my head
And attired in elegant apparel.

· · ·

You are a marvelous artist
That you could envision me in such an image, but
There's no way I could look the way you've rendered me,
Even though I'd love to.

Sure, I'll examine what you have in your hands.
This is a beautiful fabric, so soft and
Hey!
Aren't those holes in your hands,
Like they were nailed to a board?
And you're giving me this garment,
A change of clothes,
An immaculate snow-white robe! With your name inscribed on the
 hem.
I don't deserve your friendship.
You're my saving grace,
Sent from God to keep me from
Going to the grave
Looking like I spent my whole life as a worthless bum.

So is there anything I can do to return the favor?
I mean, what should I do now?
So that your gesture towards me won't be wasted
'Cause you have clothed me as a prince
To make me perfectly like the way you imagined me
In your portrait perfectly painted.

Hmm? Yes, I meant everything I just said about you.
There's no denying who you are
There never has been and never will be
Anyone as significant as you.
There's nothing wrought or wrecked by human hands
That you can't rectify.
Even when your enemies plotted to get rid of you,
You rose up to fashion a new wardrobe

For those who love your work.
You can count me as one of your faithful admirers from now on.

Okay, I promise to shred all the old stuff in my closet
I never want to be caught in faulty skins again.
But if you will advise me
I'll be clean and clad in the garb you have
Tailored and labeled for me.
And when I go out and someone
Compliments me on how I look or asks me
Where I got my clothes,
I will refer them to a copy of this
Wonderful catalog you have given me.

Yes, I will study this catalog for instructions in style
And follow its directions for the care and upkeep of
My new robes
And next time you stop by
I'll be presentable, closer to
Looking like the person in the portrait of me
You conceived, painted, and hung on my wall.

Thank you!

Pledge of Obedience Prayer

I pledge obedience to the Word
Of the Righteous Kingdom of Lord Jesus Christ
And to the promises which He has spoken:
Living in the one holy nation,
Trusting in God, innocent,
With discretion and virtue in all I say and do

By the endowment of the Holy Spirit
In Jesus's name
Amen.

Salvation Acceptance Speech

It fills me with great joy to
Walk up here and accept this prize.
I plan to keep my remarks short, for
I have no reason to brag
And only one person to thank.

Yes, please applaud loudly,
The Source of Eternal Salvation
Deserves all the thanks for this award
No other agency offers a more highly regarded trophy
In our profession
Than this blood-stained cross
Which our Prince of Peace ordains.
He gives this away so freely,
I didn't even have to do anything special—
All I had to do was agree to receive the prize when
He stood at my door and knocked and offered Himself at supper

And though I did nothing to merit this,
I consider this a treasure I can't describe
Because it confers upon me a reputation I've yet to attain myself.
This certifies that the Branch of Righteousness is next to my heart
And it justifies my life, giving me purpose, hope, and more:
I now strive to be perfect like the Apostle and High Priest of our
 profession
Because this is a reminder of the Way I received another chance.

I'd like to thank the Captain of salvation,
The first-born among many brethren,
Shepherd of the flock,
For this prize and the new life it gives me,
Giving all honor, glory and praise to God,
Whom I love.
Thank you, God bless.

Sign

A piece of liberty was delivered to me.
Didn't make any four-to-six-weeks-old phone calls
      with my credit card handy
Nor was I demanded to present COD
But the deliverer just showed up on my doorstep one day and
 knocked
And he offered it for free,
Said it was bequeathed to me a long, long time ago
And told me it's an antique with a never-diminishing value,
An heirloom millennia old,
At its inception determined I should have it

What's the catch, I asked
      No catch; it's yours: just sign for it here
I took the release form off my chest
And saw that my parcel had come certified—
The originator wanted to guarantee I received it
And the deliverer wanted to prove he delivered it.

      I, the undersigned, declare aloud in my own voice
      This indescribable gift shall be my precious cornerstone
      Wonderful, ancient of days long before I was born
      Yet has never been a tombstone beyond
      Some 36 hours about 20 centuries ago

      I, the undersigned, understand that
      I am receiving a mint condition jewel fitted for a royal crown
(Hmm, I guess that means I better remove all the junk
And all the gold and silver wannabe valuables from my vanity!)

      And I, the undersigned, find no fault
      With this gift, trusting in its authenticity
      And agree not to criticize when its liberal power
      Bathes me with light and

Miraculously transforms my shack into a temple

† _____

(Sign next to the Cross)

This is for those who require a sign.

The Esteem Poem

I am a treasure, yes I am
No matter what you think when you look at me
I am a treasure.

Maybe when you see me coming
You take off runnin' 'cause I's ugly
Maybe you think I look like they put too little
Cream in the coffee
Maybe I can't afford to buy much more than coffee
Perhaps I'm too short to dunk a basketball
And too "uncultured" to swing a golf club
Maybe I can't snap off a one-liner and break your jaw
Maybe I couldn't recognize Carol Burnett on the silver screen
If you spotted me "We're watching Carol Burnett and Friends"
Maybe I don't have letters behind my name
And perhaps you could use my nappy head to scrub a skillet
And have an electrifying experience.
Just take my image and throw it in the dumpster,
Why don't you?

No matter,
I'm still a treasure.
No, you probably wouldn't trade me
For charcoal ashes after you done grilled some t-bones,
But to Someone I'm a treasure,
A national treasure

Oh, I heard you say,
        "What makes you think so, man?"
I don't *think* so,
I **know** so.
I know because God purchased me.
He plunked down the life of His *only* Son
Jesus Christ

As the downpayment, the principal, and the interest

With that much invested, I must be a treasure
So no matter what you think when you look at me,
I am a treasure.

Jesus is a treasure, too
Priceless, all the world.
He's my today and all my tomorrows
And guess what: I didn't have to purchase Him like He did me.
He came to me free when He bought me.

Gold fades, silver tarnishes
And even I, treasure that I am
Have some spots, blemishes, imperfections.
But the Treasure that treasures me is beautiful maintenance-free
And has a value that doesn't fluctuate with the economy
Because you can't add to everything.

I'm honored that Someone so valuable
Values me,
So when He takes out His cloth
To rub me spit-n-polish clean
I just be real still for however long it takes
Because one day He'll put me on the mantel
And show me off to His guests.

Yes, I am a treasure, I am
No matter what you think when you look at me,
I am a treasure.

The Sponge
John 19:28-30; 2 Cor. 5:21

When I, a student and unofficial historian,
Survey the wondrous Cross
—Glory to God—
I see the remnant of an event that,
Yes, it saved me and allowed for my life in Christ,
But it was a horrible travesty to ever have to happen:

For the sake of a species given
Unparalleled intelligence, conscience, and compassion
But were reluctant to exercise their gifts,
The Savior, in the form of a man,
Was slandered and ridiculed,
Led like a leashed beast and hung up like a dusty scarecrow,
Endured hideous pain and embarrassment
Under the eclipsing darkness
Of His Father's eye refusing to look,
All so He could soak up all our failings, even in the then future
Like a sponge

Therefore, I,
Seventeen million five hundred thousand hours later,
Refuse to add even one more drop of vile vinegar to the sponge.
Every day I will be washed in baptismal water from
Beer-Lalohim-Zadik — the
Well Of The Holy One Who Giveth Life —
And will refrain from putting my hand to any thing
That would sully my own sponge, which must be
Squeezed out into my Savior's compassionate sacrifice
Two thousand years ago.

Go With the Flow

A small pool of clear warm water
Called out, "Come, wade in
Experience the baptism,
Take a ride to a place where the water is sweet
And your throat will never again be dry."

Someone said, "But it's so small!"
Still, I made a dash in faith,
Holding my kayak over my head,
Straight into that pool

Now a vibrant, white-water rapid river
Rushes out of my soul
And I ride, steering my kayak with my paddle

Much cleansing rain has fallen this fortnight
Fueling this rocket-rapid river.
Traveling so fast,
No machine ever devised by mankind can match it
But with the Spirit of God in me
I feel no dizziness, have complete equilibrium
And I have a large appetite for more speed.

Each day I'm hurtling faster
In a current of powerful peace.
No end in sight to this flowing giant.
Don't know where it'll lead me to
'Cause this river is mightier than me.

One thing's certain,
Don't want my kayak to wash up on shore
Where my ride'll dry up.
Have to stay in the center of this super stream
And ride the river long as it lasts.

Worth Remembering

Remember the warm waters that flowed around you?
They remember you.
Remember the gentle light that embraced you with the waters?
It remembers you.

During the heat of the day do you remember:
    The cool rainbow glow of yesterday's sunset,
    The moon's waltz over the milky stream of the sky,
    The shooting star that wiggled through a starry forest,
      to say "Hello, it's a pleasant evening,"
    The rabbits and fireflies holding silent conversations
      full of compliments,
    Or the mellow rainbow glow of this morning's sunrise

Do you remember?
Or does the hustle and bustle,
Busyness and intent of this moment
Drown out those precious moments worth remembering?

Try not to forget,
You, too, are a precious, longed-for memory.
Do you remember? the first lines of this poem?

Remember the warm waters that flowed around you?
They remember you.
Remember the gentle light that embraced you with the waters?
It remembers you.

Never forget
That even when you forget yourself
Our God, the Creator of all—
He always remembers you.

The Voice of Eden

The beautiful warbling reaches out far
Rings in your ear but seems whisper soft
From where you stand; you can't hear it
With hills obstructing the distance,
Leaves in the trees applauding,
So many jays, magpies, cuckoos, pigeons, owls
And others on their perches making their own music.

The solution?
Since the melody just won't come to your ear
You must incline your ear to the melody:
Go find it.

You know what it sounds like:
Like water flowing from diamonds.
You know where to find it,
Where you were when it discovered you,
Enraptured you, walking in the garden:
Look to the hills.

Get close, nothing between the song and you
And lock on to it with your ear
Concentrate on it as you walk
You'll still hear it miles away
As you go on in your journey.

Follow in the Trailblazer's Footsteps

Proverbs 4

Only one trail of footsteps in the sand
Leads quickly and safely across the broiling desert
It has its own cadence
Latch onto its beat with your ears,
Funneling the rhythm for your eyes to follow,
An audible rope stretched out over a deep gorge,
And then apply your best ear-eye-foot coordination.

Don't be lured away by the irregular rhythms of
Paths leading to the oases you see in the distance
Many have perished of thirst in a drunken drowsiness
By taking such a gamble.
Listen for the cadence; it will lead you far clear of those mirages.

As you follow the footsteps
That melodious cadence will peal more brightly in your ear
As if you could hear the sunrise on a beautiful June day
Hum along, let your very breaths
Answer the melody harmoniously
And your heartbeat will mimic the rhythm of your perfect steps:

Watch,
And see that your feet land squarely in the footsteps.
Don't look to the right or to the left,
Just watch your step
(And if there's a scorpion or rattlesnake
In the way up ahead, let it pass before you put your foot there
Unless you will crush its head with your foot)

Happy trails!

[*Verses:* 13-15, 18, 23, 26-27]
Jesus blazed the trail (John 14:6). He is the Trailblazer.

A Prayer to Follow

In the footsteps of Enoch and Elijah. . .
What hard places for me to go
While certainly I often send my mindflight high up toward heaven
Seeking the orbit of the eaglelion,
Their whole being, along with the eaglelion Himself,
Rose up one time, in a straight path
And never since have their bodies been seen or recovered

But sure as gravity, my mindflight always inevitably returns to the
 earth
And my body never rises more than maybe three feet
Above the surface it rests upon.
So it seems, Lord, that if I'm to rise up into heaven
You'll have to carry me, like You did with Enoch and Elijah.
So to follow in the footsteps of Elijah,
Let me examine my dreams

He walked with You.
He walked with You because he knew You were with him always
When he sat down, You were there
When he stood up, You were there
When he slept, You were there
And when he walked, You were there, keeping with his every step
And he knew it
Therefore with his every step, You lifted him a step higher
When he said, "Let it not rain," You dried up the clouds
When he said, "Let it rain fire," You sent down the flames

Do I know what Elijah knew
Or do I ask, "Where are You, Lord?"
Can I recognize what Elijah perceived?

If I paid attention, I learned from the great poet,
Who is greater, wiser, and older than Shakespeare, Milton, Hughes,

and me
That I can't go anywhere to escape Your presence.
I can climb aboard an airplane and fly above the clouds
But I will find You occupying the pilot's seat
I can descend into a submarine and dive into dark depths
But I will find You controlling the helm

. . .Right, what he wrote, those millennia ago
But my eyes are obsessed with seeing great things
My ears are stubborn about hearing grand sounds
When the gale rages, I think it's You
When the ground trembles, I think it's You
When wildfires consume, I think it's You
Obvious signs of great power, so it must be You, right?

Dig deeper,
          my muse tells me,
So I know I can hear You, Lord, since You are my muse
I can feel You in the cool breeze that kisses my cheek through my
   open window
I can see You in the beauty of a small shrub growing in the garden
I can hear You in the flashing of a firefly in the rainbow flames of a
   sunset
     My Lord, it takes a poet to dig that deep!
     But I'm just a regular person

Am I any less flesh-and-blood than Elijah?
In all of our souls there is a poet that can hear The Still Small Voice
Let this work be proof and inspiration to any of us to dig deep,
Find and concentrate on Your voice, knowing that You are here,
And follow in the footsteps of Enoch and Elijah.

First Steps

        Daddy,
Daddy,
            Where are you?

I'm trying hard as I can
To follow the sound of your
Word
            (Since I can't ever see you
            Like a big puffy cloud or
            A ball of fire in the sky)

You moved too far away from me
After you let my hands go,
Too far and I can't hear where to run
You know my developing ears have limited sensitivity
Right now.
Come back
    Please
        And take my outstretched hands
Be close to me
    Where I can hear your loving
Voice
    In my ear
                Sweet whisper

Yes,
I know you want me to   learn to walk
I know I need to   learn to walk
And one day
    Soon
I'm gonna step out
            faithfully
Towards the sound of your voice
And then

Not long after
I'm gonna take a longer walk
            And fall into your arms.
        Eventually,
                Daddy
You'll call my name
From somewhere far away
            Far as the farthest star
And I'll come runnin'

But for now
Come back
    Please
        Reach out your hand
Just inches from my outstretched hands
    And give me a
Word
    A little bit
                Louder

Then pick me up so I can
Put a big hug on your neck.

✿

Walking Prayer

Lord,
I want to take a step,
And every step I take
Step out higher on firm air
Fortified by your divine Word
Waving this world goodbye as I
Journey ever closer to your Kingdom

Jigsaw Puzzle Prayer

A day
On this earth
Is a jigsaw puzzle

Reach down
Your hand from Heaven
Lord

Put this piece
In its proper place
So that other pieces
May be joined to the solution.

Bringing the Flashlight to Its Knees

Does the light bulb know when it's browning out?
Getting dim, not letting its light shine brilliantly
And the poor souls in the tunnel strain their eyes
Looking for the end so they can rest their weary legs?

The light bulb knows when it's experienced a blackout,
It can feel the cold, recognizes its uselessness
But does it know when it's browning out
And it's time to recharge the batteries?

The light bulb, when it's browning out,
Dims so gradually, it doesn't even notice, but
He who wields the lantern can measure every lumen lost
And when the light bulb starts holding on for dear light,
To restore its power
He turns it all the way off for a moment to
Change the batteries.

Peaceful Rest
A lullaby

Before I fall asleep tonight
Make sure You tie my dreamrope tight
The eaglelion holds the rope
His strong talons carry my hope.

In my dreams I only trust Him
Adore His Word and not my whim
I hold on to the rope and wait
For all my weakness to abate

And I find my path in the right
When He gives me a crown of light
His crown of light makes me grow strong,
Heals me as I sleep all night long.

While He dangles me into rest,
In the dreams I'll climb to the crest
On the ladder of His great love
Traveling to the light above.

Full of endless power and might,
The eaglelion ends my plight:
On the back of Jesus's namesake,
I'll run strong after I awake.

At the End of the Night

It is the end of the night
And it has been dark and stormy
Heavy clouds bursting, dumping their nightmares on a tiny, young
  giant.
The stars don't shine in the middle of raindrops, honey

It has been a long, long dark night
A night so long, its dreams span from the days of
    the knights of King Arthur's court
To the cold, bitter nights after the savage
Bombing of a busy building in downtown Oklahoma City
A fortnight and three days ago

And at the end of the cold, sweaty dreams
Stands a towering night, ready to stomp on a tiny, young giant
Slumbering fitfully through torrents of rain.
The stars don't dream of shining through the raindrops, baby

This long, blue-black night grows taller with each breath
Bumping its head on the moon, high above the dreary clouds
It waves its hand and a hurricane washes Gulf of Mexico water
Up the Bayou, scattering mud up to where the Mississippi and
  Missouri
    met two years before.
A flood of memories attack dreams like a tornado
When big night twirls its finger in the jet stream

Now after all the tragedy ceases
After all the trauma fades
It is the end of the night
And no teardrops star in the dreams of a tiny, young giant, man

Because what happens at the end of the night?
It has grown too big

So big its eyes glaze over like low-lying fog when
It goes nose to nose with the sun.
And it's going to fall—
A long, long plunge
    Hurtling past the speedy Mercury   /It's gotta
                                                                 fall
    Getting scorched by the fly-trap clouds of Venus /Yes, it's
                                                               gotta fall
    Creating craters on both sides of the moon   /A long,
                                                               hard fall
    Crashing finally at the feet of the Gateway Arch
Where it becomes nothing but the caddie-shadow of a tiny, young
 giant

It is the beginning of a new day.
Time for a morning cup of coffee to start
A long, warm day, with the sun shining bright
And the sun shines all day long, yes, Lord
Yes, Lord.

✿

From The Gateway City on May 6, 1995.

70

Closet Fire

There's a fire in the closet.
Any skeletons therein are being incinerated
The invisible flame in the closet
Cannot be extinguished, but must be fed.
More powerful than a blazing cabin with a fireplace,
The closet fire calls with inescapable fumes.
Fumes with the delightful scent of incense
Which fill the air where breath is breathed,
Making sleep a festering abrasion.

When the coals are smoldering low,
It's time to rise up to kneel down inside the closet
And add fuel to the fire.

Opening

Open the blinds
Let the light bleed into my room
Too long have I slumbered in a black fog

Open the curtains
Let me see
God's glorious cloud
Overtake the dark pre-dawn sky
Like lambs' wool

Now open the window
Let me reach for the rim of the cloud
Of course I cannot grasp it
Not to worry, for it has surrounded my arm
And has firm hold of me

Then open the door
Let me walk through it
Too long I walked by the edge
Of a steep cliff, overlooking a pit
Somewhere in the depths of a dark room

Finally, Lord, open the sky
Let your blessings rain down like a warm breeze
Fill my heart like a cup of black coffee
My spirit stirs my blood and then lifts off
Rocketing to a place high above the world
Where the eaglelion soars and keeps watch
So I can sing His praises.

Morning Coffee

I am a cup
Each morning I be empty and cold after a
Night of uncertainty, hanging on a dish rack in the dark,
Just an earthquake or accident away from breaking.

But each morning
The lights come, flood me with hopeful anticipation.
And my world begins to fill up with warmth.
I am anointed by a dark, rich substance I cannot see.
An aroma surrounds me that contains sweetness.

I know that I must radiate forth
Into bright sunbeams streaming down upon me
As I am moved about by loving hands.
Soon, I am lifted up and
Touched gently by the strong lips of my Lord
And I know that I have been blessed again, this morning.

Maxim no. 44: Service

It is not low, like slavery, to be a servant of God
For if you wait on the Lord
And serve him a cup of coffee
Your tip will be of more value than the coffee,
Even richer than all the mountain-grown
    coffee beans in Colombia.

The Waiter

A consummate professional,
His first thought upon rising is to approach his patron,
Whom he humbly serves day after day,
And ask, "How may I serve You today, m'Lord?"
He is not disturbed
When his master asks him to be a receptacle
And the tables are turned.
He chews, swallows, and is filled by his master's wisdom.
Then he comes with a tray,
Heaps its contents upon his patron's plate,
Ceaselessly uttering phrases of praise and adoration
Because he is a grateful humble servant
And his master's great accomplishments are innumerable.
Patient, obedient, complaisant,
He returns to his master's table throughout the day,
Asks Him His pleasure and unhesitatingly performs His will
Never sighing or letting his shoulders droop.
Yawns do not come until night has cascaded
All the way down to his feet
At which time his master, who tips him well—
Even better than he deserves—
Bids him leave to get some rest
So his service can begin again fresh in the morning.

This Morning

How can this cup be sitting there
Filled to the brim with cold coffee —
Sharing so much in common with other cups of coffee:
Picked at the same time
Roasted, ground, brewed
At the same time,
Except it just sits there, undrunk,
A spider weaving cobwebs to hold it to the counter?

How can this cup of coffee be sitting there
When it has been bought,
Paid for?
"Waiter! Snap to!
I want that cup
                    of coffee
Bring it to my table
No, don't empty it, renew it
Heat it afresh; stir up those sluggish molecules.
Set it before me
So I may savor its steamy aroma"

So thank God
Today this cup won't just be sitting there
But it will be moved, picked up
Used
Then cleansed,
Ready to be filled again soon.

Coffee House Prayer
Psalm 143

Here is your cup of coffee,
Oh favorite patron of mine
Please enjoy it as you have always,
And then give me your usual generous tip

Please don't criticize me because my service
Could have been a little faster
Or because I couldn't find a cup with no scratches.
There isn't a waiter here who could serve you
With the perfection you deserve

I must tell you why my steps have been a little slow
To bring you your coffee this morning:
There is a bully—a thief—
Who hangs out by the door of this coffee house,
Always threatening me,
And today he beat me up, gave me a black eye,
Stole all my money and left me for dead.

Now all my muscles and bones ache
It's hard for me to walk around here
Serve folks without staggering
Or pour coffee without shaking.
I know I look like a mess.

But I think about times past
When I stood tall and firm,
Encouraged by your tremendous kindness
And instructions of wisdom
It makes me smile even through this pain

Please take my hands, steady them from trembling
Before I faint… quick, please!

Please don't be offended by my wretchedness today,
Else I get fired like a waiter who gets too many complaints
And have to beg like a bum on the corner.

Let me sit here at your table for a minute this morning
To take in the aroma of your coffee
For I know you sweeten it 'til it's perfect
Its strong vapors will invigorate me,
Put some pep in my step today.
That's why I'm waiting on you today.

And if I'm sitting at your table
When that thug comes in here
He can't get to me while you bounce him from the place

Speak to me, oh favorite patron of mine
Advise me on how to be a five-star waiter
Your reputation is renowned and lauded around the world
And I want my performance reviewer to note
That I took pointers from you

See, oh favorite patron of mine,
If you will do these things for me this morning
It won't just help me,
But it will add even more fame to your name

So please steady my hands,
Ease my pain,
And punish the creep who did this to me
Because all I want to do is serve you better each day.

Ritual Suicide

The person reading this poem is dead
(If not, then ought to be)
Rose up from a death-like state this morning
And killed himself all over again
Fell down on his knees,
Thrust through by a two-edged sword.
After the emotional jerking ceased
The puppeteer came along,
Strong, towering over the willing victim,
Strung him up—
A line attached to each hand, elbow, foot, knee,
Head and heart.
Then the puppeteer lifted the newborn marionette up,
Along with many others,
And began the puppet show.

[Lord,] show me the path of life: in Your presence is fullness of joy;
at Your right hand there are pleasures forevermore. — Ps. 16:11

Three

Enjoy the Journey

The fullness of life and love is from the Lord.

In the Zone

When it comes to poetry
And I be inspired by my Lord,
Who is my muse:

I be in a zone
Like Reggie Miller
Droppin' my man off
With a head fake and a cross-over dribble,
Rainin' jump shots like 40 days and 40 nights
(That be all season, man,
'Cluding the all-star game)
    Yak!
        Yak!
            Yak!
Don't even bother jumpin'
If you even let me get the ball
Next thing you know, it's
        Cotton!
(Love that sound!)

Silence.
It's the enemy home gym
I'm walkin' outta here with the victory
Don't have to do no trash-talkin'
'Cause my actions represented all that.

Home Court Advantage

Just imagine,
A sports arena—our modern Colosseum
Ten b-ball players—our modern gladiators—
Five of 'em in white, our heroes, the home team,
Playin' the game—our modern warfare:

Our Man, who we all came to see,
Make a move—
I mean a freak 'em, shake 'em,
Drop 'em off, break his ankle,
You lef' sumpin' on the floor move to
Da rack,
Stuff da pill down his throat,
Posterizin' 'em with a
Tomahawk monster dunk
Then take names and wave to da crowd.

Oh, don't you know we'd raise the roof!
We'd make a nap on an airport runway
Sound like a peaceful night's sleep.
An arena of sold-out praise and cheers,
And our Man,
He'd just feed off our decibels
And go into da ZONE
Wilt's hundred would look like a DNP
And Dennis Rodman would have nothin' to rebound.
By the time our Man get through,
We'd be hoarse and
His teammates look like they were horses.
The enemy team more outmatched than the
Generals vs. the 'Trotters,
So lopsided they stopped keepin' score 2000 years ago.

We're saved, so we keep comin' back for more

And every time our commotion
Lifts our Man up, puts
Him in da zone, encourages
Him
He feeds off our emotion
And keeps on doing bigger and better
Feats of heroism

The greatest cheerleader who ever lived,
If he were alive today, he'd have
A seat at center court and he'd say
Something like
"I was glad when they said unto me,
Let's go to the arena,
They havin' a pep rally."

• • •

So,
For the
One who made the bestest move I ever
Seen in my life,
This is my gift of a standing ovation.
Let it inspire
Him to bring us another victory.

✿

Written on Christmas, 1996. Partially inspired by Promise Keepers, who really know how to raise up some mighty cheers. I also want to send a shout out to my "Orange Ticket" brothers from Stand in the Gap: gettin' on target with Jesus!

"We love Jesus, yes we do! we love Jesus, how 'bout you?!!"

85

How the Champion Climbs the Rock
for Sandra C., because she loves it

A steep rock face; I'm halfway up
My arms ache, legs numb
My heart pounding in Morse code
That I need to get some rest.

A laurel tree at the top of the cliff,
Withering from oppressive August heat
In a summer hot as Nebuchadnezzar's fiery furnace,
Dropped a bundle of its glossy leaves
Which now hang precariously on a ledge
Just a few feet to my left.
I could reach it with a deft lateral move
Like Tim Hardaway's crossover dribble
But those leaves won't provide me with no shade

Restrestrestrest my heart thumps
Lungs heaving, gasping for air like
A swimmer drowning in my sweat.
Earthworms on the ground below
Climbing out of their subsoil homes
'Cause they think it's raining on them

Rest?!
My soul silences my whining body parts.
Can't you see I'm hanging on the side of a cliff?

Promise, No Idle Threat

You're quite the devil, aren't you?
Hold <u>my</u> head under water,
bring me up for a short breath
and quickly submerge my sensibilities again—
Trying to make me confess to something I don't want.

You better pray
That God doesn't give me gills
So I may breathe through this trouble—
You'll wish I was <u>only</u> Samson with a jawbone.

Looks like God, by His grace, gave me "gills" – First Corinthians 10:13

Extreme High Hurdles

Running the high hurdles on a track is easy
Now, try it with skates on a
Gravel path through a junkyard jungle,
A junkyard Doberman, foaming at the mouth
On your heels with every stride.
The path is narrow but not straight
Boulders, fallen trees, thorny weeds, barbed wire
And broken-down, can't-take-you-nowhere-no-more-man auto-
 mobiles
Litter your way.
Should you decide to go around instead of get over,
The punishment is severe:
How does getting chewed up by hot, vicious jaws sound?
Sounds like hell to me.
Better strap on your helmet, slip on knee pads and elbow pads
And prepare for the ride of your life
You got no choice,
And this ain't no video game or virtual reality—
One life is all you get.

No teammates, no opponents, no clock to race
Getting through the course is its own reward
For at the end you get to meet the king of the course.
There's no need to ask him why the course is there
Just thank him you finished the race and will never
Have to go through it again.

How the Champion Is Champion

What about
When the champion rock climber
Just can't pull himself no higher?

Hanging on the side of a cliff
Not possible to convert vertical rock
Into soft horizontal mattress with down-filled pillows,
But even though his mind barks out
"Just a little bit further!
There's a ledge just above my hands:
Come on, get up!"
Quadriceps, biceps, and triceps,
Hamstrings, glutes, and delts
Refuse to perform his will, they go on strike.

Toeholds slip away, legs dangle
Fingers throb, shoulders on fire
Sweat lubricates his hand holds
And if he loses his grip
This height he's conquered
Will rise up and crush every bone in his body

What then?
He must summon the courage and gasp
To alert his Climbing Partner,
The one who suggested he climb this rock
(Who, in fact, designed the rock face,
Knowing the champion's limits)
And is already up on the ledge waiting for him

The Partner will look down upon him and say
"I will not forsake you and let you fall
Let go of your hand hold with your right hand
And take hold of my ample hand.

I will pull you up to this ledge
Where you can rest until you're ready to climb further."

Missing the Boat
for Rachel

I stood alone on the pier for many years
It seemed like a lifetime
I got frozen, battered, cooked, refrigerated
Many times over while I waited—
Why oh why did I go for love's bait?

In the meantime I saw many boats—
Dhows, small dahabeahs, sampans,
Gondolas, canoes, dinghies, and sometimes
A romantic little catamaran—
Take passengers and float out towards the Sea of Love.
I was always improperly accompanied, they said.

Finally, you came to wait with me
You were a mermaid, a princess from some griot's tale,
But you were real.
Oh, we built an ardent rapport while we waited
And no way any boat would refuse us.

A soft melody filled the air
As our personal ferry neared the dock.
Suddenly, you decided to take another
Route to the Sea of Love,
But I could not answer your calling
And could only sadly watch
As you dove gleefully into the bay.

I couldn't risk swimming after you
But now I stand on this pier, alone again
Praying I didn't miss my boat.

The Cat's Tale

I'm not a natural mouser
I'm not one of those cats who needs
An entire wall to contain his tally marks.
I used to envy those cool creatures
That can catch scores of mice
Any week they choose

But it's not like I haven't had my taste of a mouse.
It took me a long time,
But I finally caught one after a long chase.
Oh, I enjoyed that meal!
I savored it like fresh salmon on a bed of chipped ice.
Most cats would have devoured it and
Begun another short chase.

Unfortunately, that picnic came to an end.
But I'm patient, letting the flavor linger in my memory
While I sit back,
Confident that I can catch another one.
But I'm beginning to get hungry
My paws twitch in my sleep and my hairs stand on end

If I don't chase something soon—
Whether or not I catch it—
They'll be taking me to a pet psychiatrist.
In the end I won't settle for a ball of yarn,
I'm waiting for that giant every mouser dreams of.
When it comes along, I'm gonna catch it.
I promise its death will be painless
And then it can deliciously nurture me for the rest of my cozy life.

The Old Dog's Tale

for the memory of Alonzo (Lonnie), my family's Old English Sheepdog

I know a good many dogs
Who will chase anything that moves
Cats, squirrels, birds—
Rabbits'll tie 'em in knots—
Frisbees and tossed balls
And an occasional car.
Oh, and if they catch their own tail wagging
Out of the corner of their eyes,
They'll run around in dizzying circles for hours
With growls of satisfaction in their throats.

Me,
I've never been into that foolishness.
Oh, sure, in my younger days
On rare occasions I'd run after something,
Just to see if I were capable
But it was always something I couldn't catch.
Rabbits were too quick, cats too sneaky, and
Birds in the bushes
Shoot, they had one up on me — they could fly!

(I did catch something once:
The sweetest little shrew
But my master wouldn't let me keep it
So I have no trophy to brag about when I go to the kennel)

Nowadays
These old bones don't get up for nothin'
Unless somebody caught it for me, killed it, and
Deposited it into my food dish.

I let the rabbits bound all around me
And play in the garden all day long.

I just yawn and stretch out my furry front paws
Let my master handle them
And if a cat should wander by and then
Dart off, trying to tempt me into a chase,
I might raise my head, go
Woof!
And go back to my nap

And when I want some satisfaction
I whine a little bit or howl at the moon
Then they come to me and pet my head
Or rub my belly
While I just let my tongue hang out to the side

So who needs a chase?

The Glove

(No, even though I love hoops
I am not Gary Payton
If I were, this probably would not be written.)

The left hand doesn't have to know what the right hand is doing
But what the left hand is wearing
Would like to know what the right hand is wearing.

I have not seen, yet
But I know what's on the other hand is a perfect match for me
'Cause the magnificent being whose hand I'm on
Is all about perfection.
Didn't you know? Haven't you seen his moves?
Like they say, If you don't know, you better ask somebody!
He can go to his left with such a freaky move
You'll get dropped off back in Sunday School as a kid
Askin' a question like, "Don't they wear gloves in *baseball*?"
This is one who'll make Air Jordan keep his tongue in his mouth.

I've seen some of his matchless miraculous moves
Even been privileged to be on hand when he's made some
But what I'm really looking forward to
Is when warm-ups are over and the tip-off has been won:
Watch me — I mean *him* — score, with a sweet-georgia-brown
  fingeroll
That'll make George "Only-the-Iceman-may-fingeroll" Gervin shut
  his mouth

And then, after the enemy has turned it over, this
God on the court
Will clap his hands to call for the rock.
Yes, yes — that's when I'll get to meet my mate:
Just like me but not exactly
'Cause one hand isn't the other hand, though shaped in nearly

identical fashion.
We'll cradle the ball together, our joint responsibility.

Now you know.
See ya at the game.

○

These past four poems are aimed particularly at young people (and anyone not married). If I may get on my soapbox, did you know that it's possible to have friendships with members of the opposite sex without any intimate physical contact and enjoy that much more than the alternative? I found out by experience. Save your passion for your God-given soulmate, and you'll cherish the relationship so much more.

Blowing Kisses Back

An invisible cloud hangs overhead
Filling the dusk air with a glowing smile
And holding hands with my spirit

Actually much more than a cloud
But my limited imagination can't find the words to frame Him

Anyway, I turn west on my way home
A beautiful skyscape leaps through my windshield,
A blown kiss that
Smooches me right in my face

It's hard to keep my eyes on the road
Three pretty, puffy giants tower over the horizon
Silhouetted against a background as red as my blushing face

Now, normally I balk at public displays of affection
And send out a PDA alert,
But it's hard to be unresponsive to this kind of love

His love is on display for everyone to see
Though some choose to ignore it
But I gratefully blow back a kiss of praise.

Poet Laureate of the Swamp

I know a poet who is a natural
In the same league as Shakespeare, Milton, Hughes, Dunbar
Johnson, Sandburg, Dickinson, Angelou, Dove,
And any laureate you can name from the
Mostly useless-and-forgotten literature courses
They bombarded you with in school.
In fact, gifted inspiration courses through him
Like the Psalms of David

But while millions or more have read the greats,
This fella's work clings to a dying tree
Seen by few: like a playground hoops star
Who never made the in be a,
Even though he has a be a
'Cause the changing winds never came,
To sweep him away in the flow of the right victories

It's all because of his skins.
Skins of sins,
As we call it here in this jungle.
They're not fair, smooth,
Pleasing to the eye or touch,
But thin, scaly, flaky and filthy.
Layers of skin accumulate, weigh him down
And he's slow to shed them.
When he does, it's not enough

Man, this fella could go places,
See the lushest, most vibrant regions of the forest
Even climb Jacob's ladder
And be seen in his best, most regal skins
If he would just stop putting off his
Regular visits to the eaglelion.
The King will ask him just one question:

"Do you love Me more than these. . . ?"
And after he answers affirmatively,
His Majesty will spread those majestic wings with
Plumes the color of blood
And with three wingbeats create mighty winds of change
'Til every false skin is blown away
And he glistens like fresh snow.

The Larva

Stepped away from my cooling car for a stroll
On a moist chilly May evening.
When I returned, I found a cryptic message
Scrawled across the dewy top for me.

Thought a UFO had landed and left me a memo
Regarding my destiny
But this long, spiraling word was still growing
Right before my eyes!

I peered close with a spotlight
Looking for the author of this curious writing.
There was my alien—all of half an inch long,
Green, with lots of spots for hair, and more legs than I could count
Bobbing up and down with a gross hitch from head to rear
While slowly moving forward—whichever way that happened to
 be that moment

It was making a monumental masterpiece on the top of my vehicle
After dropping down from the underside of a leaf—way back
 home.
It had stowed away all that distance
To share its inspiration with me.

"Life is a strange adventure
You never know where you may go
Focus on God's authentic love
And let your true message flow."

Dedicated to a Dying Tree

It was late in the night
When all the world was asleep
But me… and the sky.
I walked outside as my dog ran in the house
Away from the lightning that flashed in the north.
I sauntered around my backyard.
My mind was burdened by
Slow, anguished thoughts.
A tree is dying in my yard.
The poor thing is green on only half
And there are places where the
Trunk is smooth, barkless,
With insects crawling there.
I smashed the bugs with my foot—
How dare they torture something
As precious as a tree in my yard?
A tree that has held birds, me, dreams,
For two-thirds of my life—
A dying tree.
There aren't many trees left in my yard—
Just two of six.
Now I feel deep down the agony
Of this tree as it loses its vitality.
The lightning sheds light upon glimpses of mortality.
But… this tree is young—as am I,
But it's fading away— will I?
I ran my hand along the naked part
Of the tree, and I made it a promise.
It may soon experience death,
But I won't experience a death with it,
And all the dreams it held for years—
I will mold them into seeds
And raise a vibrant, lush forest.

Colonels of Corn
Prov. 11:30,28,27,26,25,24

There are two trees in my life

One of them, gnarly, is not worth examining
It lies on the ground without root
Had cared only to accumulate lovebird nests
And collect the exotic plumes
Without supporting the eggs and hatchlings
With shady leaves and nourishing fruit on its branches.

How many such sick, fallen trees can you find in a forest?
I'd rather talk about my pure corn tree. . . .
Don't laugh: it's unique; that's why you haven't heard of its variety

Pure corn is what the tree is about
Its intent is to feed any who is hungry
And whenever juicy corn is plucked
That branch grows larger and more venerable

This tree is an army fighting a holy war
Like the Tribe of Judah.
Its kernels of corn are its ammunition
Biological weapons that are not lethal,
But enrich the lives of the affected.

And whenever a battle is won
Someone prevails to obtain an ear of corn wet with juice
And the branch that fired the fateful volley
Is commended with the command rank of colonel
By the lion (king/general) who sits alert in the midst of the tree
Like it's his throne.

Colonels of corn are decorated by dew
When the morning star shines brightly.

Prayer From a Fiery Furnace

Will You hold me up?
This smoldering smoke gets in my eyes
All I hear is the worrisome crackle.
The heat is getting to me
I'm scared!

Before I was banished to this infernal suit
The only flames I saw were the inspiring leaves of autumn
And I was thankful for how my life was changing colors,
Looking forward to seeing pristine blessings patter down softly,
But now white-hot blazes have me in darkness
And if there's any way out of here, I can't see it
I'm scared!

There are horrible tongues all over this place
Threatening to lick my skin with razor-sharp barbs.
They don't whisper, they roar   laughter
Guffawing at my circumstances,
Not caring I did nothing to deserve being in hot water,
Chattering constantly that I'm gonna burn.
I'm scared!

I'm neck-deep in my boiling sweat,
For which I can't find a shut-off valve.
The flames don't care if I don't make eye contact
Because not just my eyes but my whole body
Waters up involuntarily
And I'm afraid I'll blink   out
I'm scared!

I'm not afraid to admit it, that I'm scared.
This is no myth or fairy tale
I can't call on no impervious-to-fire comic-book hero
So will You hold me up, that I don't drown in these flames?

I've called on You before, and You've never failed to
Send someone to encourage me, to strengthen my hands
But this time I'm *really* in a bind; my hands are tied.
If there's any escape for me I can't make it on my own.

Whatever is cooking in this molten life
Let some good come out of it so that millions
Can recognize who You are and how good You are
Pop my kernels of corn so that the poor can buy
And be satisfied.
And distribute the wages of my crop among my
Loved ones: parents, wife and children, brothers and sisters
So they'll know that Your love for them is so great,
My love for them is just a kiss from You.

Okay, I'm not so scared anymore.
It's hard to save a drowning swimmer who refuses to relax
I'll stretch out on my back; I'll breathe
But will You hold me up?
The heat's getting to me.

Words of the Last One In

Daniel 3:25

I most certainly will hold you up
I will be your thermal protection
I will absorb the heat.

You see, they really wanted to throw
Me in here. I was their true target
But I was beyond their grasp
So they held you for ransom
And here I am

I most certainly will hold you up
I will be your thermal protection
I will absorb the heat.

Just keep doing what you're doing.
Relax; we'll sweat it out together
The flames will continue to be seven times seven
Times hotter than your flesh can handle
And will continue to be a daunting, blinding blaze, but

I most certainly will hold you up
I will be your thermal protection
I will absorb the heat.

And your being in the fire will have no power over you
Not one hair of your head will be singed
Your clothes will remain clean and fresh
They won't even smell smoke on you
Because

I most certainly will hold you up
I will be your thermal protection
I will absorb the heat.

•••

I will take their flames and
Execute perfect enthalpy
They'll see me in the vision of the fire they put you in
But still won't be able to lay hands on me.
Your patience in the flame will bring fame to my name.

I most certainly am holding you up
I am all the thermal protection you need
I have been, am, and will be taking the heat.

The Reporters

A war broke out in heaven
This should not be news to you
Because the conflict has already been decided.
The resolution and the institution of peace
Have been covered in <u>The Gospel</u>.
The colonels of corn were not in the skirmish;
Their battle is different:
They are reporters in charge of covering stories
As the reigning Prince in power keeps the peace,
Establishing order and introducing reforms around the globe.

The movie version has already been scripted.
Many people have seen and *loved* it.
One of the colonels gave it one of its many rave reviews.

I hope none of you readers, loyal or new
Takes offense to my expressing an opinion
(Which some may feel is not unbiased;
Still, have faith in my journalistic integrity, please),
But, to be honest
The editor-in-chief is proud of his colonels of corn
And hopes one or more of them wins
A Pulitzer or Nobel
For excellence in serving <u>The Gospel</u>.

How the Champion Lives
Psalm 26

I'd like to know what you think
After all, you are my Climbing Partner.
Don't you think I've been climbing like a champion
Just the way you trained me?
I haven't faltered,
And I won't slide back down this rock.
Check my support rope. Give it a firm tug
To make sure my grappling hook is securely embedded in the rock

You have been caring and thoughtful, Partner,
Leading me up a course excellent for reaching the top
I'm diligent to use the hand holds and toeholds you utilized.

Didn't you choose me to accompany you on this expedition
Because I don't sit around with other rock climbers
Bragging about past performances or exaggerating my talents?
I'd gotten tired of that nonsense and quit hanging around.
The only thing that matters is my existing challenge
And how I will meet it with honest dedication.
I'd like to walk around the top of the highest of heights,
Where you have been and named in your honor.

When I get there
I'm going to shout until the canyons echo with your name.
The story of how you brought me to the pinnacle of my life,
How you designed this awesome rock face for me,
How you encouraged me to have the courage to climb over my
 doubts,
How you led me and guided me
Will carry my gratitude the way the wind carries a wing feather
And people will hear it down in the valleys.

Partner, I'm headed towards your summit

But I already love its cozy hospitality
'Cause you live there and have invited me to come and stay
And I'm trying to get there so I can see all your trophies.

Please don't let me slip off course and slide back
To the ground to join all those who've slipped up,
Fallen down with scrapes and bruises.
Some of them will try to pull me off the rock
And offer me a "great" "opportunity" to promote their causes
By pretending to find it a challenge to scale their inferior stones.

No, Partner, I promise to climb up in your path
As long as you find it worthwhile to be my guide.
Please be patient with me if I start to lag or tire,
But right now my grip is as sure and steady as a champion
As I anticipate mingling with the other
Champions you've trained and coached
And talking about what you've done for me.

The Story of a Great Journey

I am a great nation
Which traveled through a desert
And as I walked—on
Footsteps already laid out before me—
This sweet bread and savory meat rained
Like manna from heaven
It dripped from my ears
And filled up my path

A remarkable substance, this provision
Which fell into my hands without my having to labor for it
And spread out before me like a king's feast
We gathered it and it nourished our soul
The way a good book will keep you up turning pages all night
Oh, man! was it sweet! Sweet like passionfruit juice
It accumulated before me as I walked
So I was not belly-aching throughout the trek across the desert.
Come to think of it, my mouth never got dry, either.
And energy! Never had so much in my life
Could've run through a mountain and made it move.
Can't quite explain what got into me, but it's clear
I am a nation dwelling in a wonderful new homeland.

I made sure I stayed in line with the steps in front of me,
Eating the tasty meat I picked up from each
Little well of profundity perfectly suited to my foot
Like honey in honeycomb.
So satisfying, like completing a chore you had to do
And then gulping bug juice like your life depended on it:
Loved it to the last drop.

Sweet, sweet bread and tender, juicy meat, perfectly seasoned
Sustained me through my journey
Kept my rations of water full and made my blood flow

As if I had another heart pumping.
If I'd gashed my wrist
Blood could've sprung like Old Faithful from a never-closing
  wound
And I'd still be going today
It's amazing! I hope you follow me, 'cause I can't quite explain:
It's like, not my own blood; can't you see that much?
It must've been that sweet bread and savory meat giving me a
  transfusion.

The further I went, following in the footsteps
And the more I ingested and digested
And the stronger the blood pumped through my veins
The keener my eyes became
It looks to me like the sun shines even at night
So much sunlight has splashed on me and flowed through me
Surely I must be full and glowing with
Light that changes the way things look.
I certainly saw new things, and they weren't mirages
My steps led me through a door
A door (?) in the middle of the desert.

As the light swept me along the steps in the sand
It ushered me through the door
Brought me face to face with a shepherd
Whose face had a great glow of twelve stars as close as our sun
I found life about me and realized what had just happened:

A dead man walking through a dead desert
Passed through the door of his tomb
And saw that he was standing in an edenic pasture,
Sheep as far as the eye could see,
Looking alive at the face of the voice who loudly called him

I looked at my hands, which are covered by new skin:
The old layers fell away like discarded snakeskin

A similar shedding happened at my feet
And I danced to loose my ankles from the shackles of flesh
And my face. . .
I can't see myself, but I can feel my cheeks glowing
In reaction to being so close to someone so great

He spoke to me and
Mm-mm! Voice tasted like fresh cinnamon rolls and succulent
 sirloin
He said:
        I have broken myself into pieces
        And led you across a harsh desert land
        Like drawing a sparrow with bread crumbs
        You ignored the footsteps of emptiness
        That led to mirages of immediate meals of dainty meats
        And faithfully gathered me, bit by bit
        Because you believed a greater feast awaits you
        Now you stand here with me in paradise
        Knowing that the vision which drove your journey
        Has honestly come to pass as promised.
        Your life is just beginning.
        And you will live like kings in kings' mansions
        And everything you eat will taste like
        Sweet bread and savory meat.
        Just stay here with me.

So I'll stay—you bet
Understanding that you'd remain in perfect health and never taste
 of the grave,
Who would turn down unlimited chocolate cake and prime rib
After all, aren't you what you eat?
My path of footsteps through the desert
Has turned into a vine in a pasture of plenty
And I am a nation dressed in lambskin
Dedicated to composing grapes of grace,
The favorite commodity of the shepherd who runs this

Land in which I dwell with peace

And it's all because of the sweet bread and savory meat—
Which the wind fed me along the way—
That I am here
As I have told you from the beginning.

Spirits Rising

Standing on the bank of a river in winter
Normally a hawk would nip my ears, screaming
Today sits on my shoulder, feathers lightly ruffled
I can see it in the wavy reflection from the river mirror,
As not-cold raindrops make the water move.
I see my face — not clearly, but definitely there
The raindrop-ripples curl around my smile
As they reach up and nibble my toes through my boots

When the river reaches my knees, I lean to the right
When the currents tickle my belly, I wade to a rock
When the tide massages my neck and shoulders,
I stretch out on my back and float with the flow

A rainbow circles the azure sky
A warm glow invites me east
And as I float past the tip of Mt. Kilamanjaro,
Which is quickly disappearing underwater,
The eaglelion takes flight to usher my baptized body
As it floats and rises through the rainbow gate
Into the palace of my Lord.

High Hurdles

He was with me on the starting blocks
Before the gun went off
Didn't hear the shot, though
'Cause He told me when to launch my body
It was easy at first, like taking baby steps,
But then the first one came up in my path

He was with me when I jumped
I sprang up like a trampoline in my shoes
Smiled as I saw nothing in front of me
As I flew through the air
That was not too tall for me, I thought

He was with me when my soles touched down
I heard His barked cadence whispered in my ear
Guiding the placement of my feet
In regimented fashion
My strides a military metronome

And each time another one came up in my path
He was there, putting spring in my step
I got over, no matter how tall it stood

And He was with me as I crossed the finish line,
Breaking the tape
So on the high podium, I said
This gold medal belongs to You.

Words of Gratitude

First I thank my Father in heaven, my Lord Jesus Christ, and my helper, the Holy Spirit, for without Them I could not do anything.

I praise God for the following persons He has put in my life.

My parents, my brother Todd, my grandmother . . . we're a small family, but we're held together by love. Let's get closer yet. Your love has largely shaped who I am. I hope and pray that I have made and will make you proud of me. . . . Also, Aunt Tommie, Ricardo, Donnita, Shanita, and all my second cousins . . . I love you and you're in my prayers. Congratulations, Ricardo, on your marriage to Constance! It was a beautiful wedding and you have a beautiful wife. 'Right folks, who's next?!

All my brothers and sisters at Riverview Church of God, St. Louis, Mo. . . . thank you for all the spiritual enrichment, direction, love, and prayers. This would not have been possible without you. Thank you, Sis. Sandy, for pointing me home.

My literature and writing instructors at the University of Missouri-St. Louis: Charles Wartts, Judi Linville, Ellie Chapman, Linda Kick, Ronn Hopkins (just one semester — where'd you go, man?), Howard Schwartz, Steve Schreiner, and Shirley LeFlore . . . Y'all did good, if I must say so myself! God bless you all. Special thanks to Ms. LeFlore for being an instrument by which God has honed my craft. Also, much thanks to Dr. Bridgette Jenkins for an understanding ear.

Sandra Clerk, Rob Shaviss, Michael Tapp, Jacque Becton . . . you taught me a lot.

Jane Neukomm, Judy Dowd, Charles Duffy, Jane Lunneman, Karen Price, Charles Edmond, Coach Bob Pikula, Vernon Mitchell, and Hon. Jimmie Edwards at Berkeley Senior High School . . . you helped put some sense in me before I even knew I could capture poetry, and I hope I can make Berkeley proud of the Bulldog — I mean *man* — you helped shape. William Miller . . . thank you for the wisdom you handed down to me as my Sunday School teacher as I was growing up.

The Urban League Vaughn Culture Center, Ngoma! at La Patisserie, Garrett Gallery, River Styx at Duff's . . . thank you for the forums to expose the St. Louis poetry circle to me and me to it.

There are numerous entertainers (that includes college and pro athletes) whom God has blessed with talents which they offer, thereby making our lives more enjoyable. Whether they intend to or not, they minister to us by doing what they love to do. There are too many for me to name all those whose efforts brighten my life, so I won't try — plus, I'm acquainted with very few and am close friends with none of you. Nevertheless, if you're reading this and are in an entertainment business, take a moment to reflect on the effects you have on the lives of ordinary people. You just might be making somebody's life brighter, even if not many people like or appreciate what you do. God rewards you for your work (or play) — if He doesn't find any fault with what or how you do — because He is using you to bless His people. Anyway (I don't mean to "preach" in my words of gratitude, only to tell the truth), I pray that my offering here has the same day-brightening effect on the lives of you, my readers, as entertainers have on my life.

Thanks to Bro. Stanley for the reminder of what "BIBLE" stands for.

Todd C. . . . you been my homey since before I ever got them unwanted nicknames (you know which ones I'm talking about!) — well before I ever thought about writing poems. Maurice, ol' pal . . . where you been? Let's do lunch sometime (or invite me over). Rachel . . . it was partly because of you that I wrote my first poem. I'll always treasure the friendship we had. Stay in touch. Anissha . . .I've learned a lot about being a friend from you. You mean a lot to me, even though none of the poems I've written to tribute you were chosen for this book. I guess none of them fit. I promise to get you in the next book, "Lady A." But if you're in a hurry to see your name in print, you could publish your own book, because you're a better poet than I am! I know someone who might publish it!

A big thank you to all of you who have read this book. I pray that something has touched you, made a positive difference in your life. Please let me know how you feel.

To the "mysterious unmatched glove" . . . it's almost time for tipoff! Thanks for waiting and praying for me.

June 1999

www.ingramcontent.com/pod-product-compliance
Lightning Source LLC
Chambersburg PA
CBHW072027040426
42447CB00009B/1772